OVERCOMING ADVERSITY:
SHARING THE AMERICAN DREAM

CARRIE UNDERWOOD

MASON CREST PUBLISHERS
PHILADELPHIA

OVERCOMING ADVERSITY:
SHARING THE AMERICAN DREAM

CARRIE UNDERWOOD

MARIKA JEFFERY

MASON CREST PUBLISHERS
PHILADELPHIA

ABOUT CROSS-CURRENTS

When you see this logo, turn to the Cross-Currents section at the back of the book. The Cross-Currents features explore connections between people, places, events, and ideas.

Produced by OTTN Publishing, Stockton, New Jersey

Mason Crest Publishers
370 Reed Road
Broomall, PA 19008
www.masoncrest.com

First printing

1 3 5 7 9 8 6 4 2

Library of Congress Cataloging-in-Publication Data

Jeffery, Marika.
  Carrie Underwood / Marika Jeffery.
     p. cm. — (Sharing the American dream : overcoming adversity)
  Includes bibliographical references.
  ISBN 978-1-4222-0599-0 (hardcover) — ISBN 978-1-4222-0763-5 (pbk.)
  1. Underwood, Carrie, 1983——-Juvenile literature. 2. Singers—United States—Biography—
Juvenile literature. I. Title.
  ML3930.U53J44 2008
  782.421642092—dc22
  [B]
                                2008036573

OVERCOMING ADVERSITY:
SHARING THE AMERICAN DREAM

TABLE OF CONTENTS

CHAPTER ONE

A NASHVILLE NIGHT TO REMEMBER

On November 6, 2006, Carrie Underwood prepared for the 40th annual Country Music Association (CMA) Awards. These awards honor the most talented artists in country music. And for the first time, Carrie was one of the nominated musicians. It was a dream come true for this young singer, who had grown up admiring many past CMA Award winners. Now Carrie hoped to join their ranks herself.

Country Music's Biggest Night

Carrie's fame was still relatively new. Her path to the CMAs had begun less than two years earlier when she auditioned for season four of the televised singing competition *American Idol*. The purpose of this show was to find up-and-coming singers. Each week, the *American Idol* contestants sang songs on live television. Three judges—Randy Jackson, Paula Abdul, and Simon Cowell—then critiqued these performances. After the show was over, viewers voted for their favorite singer, and the contestant with the fewest votes was sent home. This continued each week until only one talented person remained. At the end of season four, that talented person was Carrie.

Since winning *American Idol*, Carrie had become an internationally recognized celebrity. And now, she was nominated for

Carrie Underwood pauses for photos on the red carpet at the Country Music Association awards ceremony in November 2006. The young singer was thrilled to be nominated for several important awards.

four CMA Awards. Two of those nominations were for her hit song "Jesus, Take the Wheel." Her third nomination was for Female Vocalist of the Year. Her fourth nomination was for the special Horizon Award. The Horizon Award is given each year to the new artist who showed the most career development and growth.

The 2006 CMA Awards ceremony was held at the Gaylord Entertainment Center in Nashville, Tennessee. Nicknamed "Music City," Nashville is famous for its country music heritage. Concert halls and recording studios line the streets, and many country music stars make their homes nearby.

READ MORE

Read "The Country Music Association" to learn more about the organization that distributes the CMA Awards each year. Go to page 44.

Everyone in Nashville— including Carrie, of course— was excited about the evening. After all, the CMAs were dubbed "Country Music's Biggest Night." Perhaps with a little luck, Carrie would be able to call it her biggest night, too.

Carrie Takes Center Stage

Carrie arrived at the CMA Awards escorted by her friend and former *American Idol* contestant, Anthony Fedorov. As the two Idol celebrities walked down the red carpet, all eyes were on Carrie and her gorgeous platinum-colored gown. The dress was worth $850,000 because of the nearly 800 diamonds set in its straps. Designer David Rodriguez and the company Kwiat Diamonds had created this gown especially for Carrie. But this dress was more than a stunning work of art; it had been created for a special purpose. After the CMA Awards were over, the dress would be auctioned for charity. Some of the proceeds would go to Carrie's favorite organization, the

Carrie performs her hit "Before He Cheats" at the 2006 CMA show.

Humane Society, as well as Kwiat's chosen charity, the Make-A-Wish Foundation.

During the awards ceremony, Carrie sang her hit single "Before He Cheats." For this performance, she changed into a gold, sequined mini-dress that glittered on stage. White-hot lights blazed behind her as she belted out the song to a packed theater. It was a powerhouse performance that impressed her country music peers.

Later that evening, Carrie anxiously waited for one of the biggest announcements of the night—the award for Female Vocalist of the Year. This was the one honor Carrie truly wanted—the one that symbolized so much to her as an artist.

READ MORE

To learn more about one of Carrie Underwood's hits, read "The Lowdown on 'Before He Cheats'" on page 45.

The four other nominees were Sara Evans, Faith Hill, Martina McBride, and Gretchen Wilson. Each was a country music veteran with a long and distinguished career. Three of them had even won the Female Vocalist award in the past.

A Tense Moment

When it finally came time to reveal the winner, all five nominated women waited anxiously. And then came the big announcement. The Female Vocalist of the Year was . . . Carrie Underwood!

Amazed and overjoyed, Carrie stood up and hugged Anthony. This was one of the biggest moments in her life! Tears streamed down her face as she walked on stage and received her award. Then she gave her acceptance speech, brimming with happiness:

> Two years ago, I was sitting at home watching these very awards, watching all these other people win and have the best nights of their lives, and this is the best night of my life. And I have had so many, so many good times and so many wonderful things happen to me this past year. . . . Thank you so, so much. Oh my gosh!

Carrie Underwood was on top of the world. Her dream had become a reality. To top it all off, later that night Carrie won the

Horizon Award, one of the most distinguished awards for new artists. It was an amazing night that Carrie would never forget.

Have a Little Faith

With so much good news, it might have seemed like nothing could have gone wrong. But one little incident made headlines. During the presentation of Female Vocalist of the Year, nominee Faith Hill seemed visibly upset that Carrie had won. In front of the camera, Faith threw up her hands, screamed "What?" and marched off. To the public, it looked like an outburst of anger. But Faith insisted afterwards it was meant as a joke. "The idea that I would act disrespectful towards a fellow musician is unimaginable to me," Faith said in a statement. "Carrie is a talented and deserving female vocalist of the year."

After the 2006 CMAs, Carrie excitedly shows off her two awards: for Female Vocalist of the Year and the Horizon Award given to an up-and-coming performer.

This incident created quite a scandal, but Carrie understood it was simply a joke gone wrong. More importantly, the real excitement for Carrie still remained the awards themselves. Even before her CMA win, Carrie had become a part of the country music community. "Country radio, the fans, they have been great," Carrie said in the summer of 2006. "They didn't view me as an outsider and took me in right away. I've been very fortunate to get the right mix of people working with me." Now that she had won two CMA awards, the country music community knew that Carrie Underwood was here to stay.

CHAPTER TWO

A COUNTRY GIRL AT HEART

Carrie Marie Underwood was born on March 10, 1983, in Muskogee, Oklahoma, and grew up in the nearby town of Checotah. In Checotah, a small town with a population of 3,500, Carrie lived on a farm with her father, Steve, and her mother, Carole. Carrie also has two older sisters—Shanna, who is twelve years older, and Stephanie, who is nine years older.

The Underwoods were a close-knit family. Steve worked as a paper mill employee and a cattle rancher, while Carole taught in a local elementary school. Together, both parents strived to give their three daughters a loving, happy home. The family was active in their Baptist church, and all three girls were raised with strong moral values. Carrie was also deeply influenced by her mother. "She is wonderful," Carrie said. "She has done everything she could to make sure I had everything I needed."

Carrie loved the Oklahoma countryside and spent a lot of her childhood exploring the great outdoors. "I definitely was a tomboy," she declared. "I climbed trees, and I'd jump hay bales and play with the cows, and Dad would take me fishing." Carrie also liked to search for four-leaf clovers in the grass. Whenever she found one (and she found many), she would always wish for the same thing—to one day become famous.

Oklahoma governor Brad Henry (center) and his wife Kim (left) present Carrie Underwood with a replica of a road sign to be placed in her hometown after she won the *American Idol* competition in May 2005.

Born to Sing

Carrie first started to sing at her family's church when she was just three years old. Meanwhile, her sisters, Shanna and Stephanie, were also introducing Carrie to 1980s hard rock. "One of my earliest memories was singing Mötley Crüe's 'Smokin' in the Boys Room' when I was five," Carrie said.

Carrie looked up to her older sisters and listened to a lot of the same music they did. But being a little kid, Carrie didn't always sing the songs the right way. Later, she recalled:

> When I was little, I would put on my headphones, and I would rock out, and sing the wrong words to

every single song. My sister would get so mad at me, like, "Mom, she's ruining the song again." And mom would always yell back, "Let her sing it any way she wants to."

It didn't matter to Carrie that she got the words wrong. What mattered was the music—and the fun of singing!

In her parents' car, Carrie also listened to country tunes on the radio. Country music was a big part of Oklahoma culture, and Carrie quickly became a fan. Some of her favorite artists included Reba McEntire, Martina McBride, and Randy Travis. Once country crept into Carrie's heart, it grew into a true musical passion.

Performing in the Spotlight

Performing was always a big part of Carrie's life. In elementary school, she participated in plays and musicals. Then, at age 10, she started singing with her church choir. By seventh grade, Carrie was entering talent contests and competitions at county fairs. She never won first place, but this didn't matter to her. "I didn't need to win," she said. "If I got third and got a little trophy or money for school, that made me happy."

One of Carrie's biggest supporters was her mom, Carole. Often, it was Carole Underwood who made Carrie's performance costumes. Carrie would wear these flashy outfits with big, teased hair and lots of makeup. Then she would go out on stage and perform like a real country music star.

Carrie was not just a talented singer. She could also play the guitar and piano. She

READ MORE

Read "Country Music 101" to learn more about this musical genre. Go to page 46.

Carrie (center) poses with her parents, Carole and Steve Underwood, during a 2007 charitable event.

worked hard and continued to compete, hoping to one day get "discovered." It was her dream to sing professionally.

Then, around the age of 13, she was given the chance to make a demo, a recording that could be played for record companies looking for talented new singers. It was a great opportunity, and Carrie hoped it would lead to a music career. She traveled all the way to Nashville to record some songs. But unfortunately, the record companies showed no interest in her demo.

In retrospect, Carrie is glad. Fame and fortune would have been hard for a 13-year-old to handle. "I honestly think [now] it's a lot better that nothing came out of it, because I wouldn't have been ready then," she later said. Fortunately for Carrie, the future had better things in store.

Living the Life of a Good Girl

In high school, Carrie studied hard and earned good grades. She and her friends were part of a wholesome crowd that liked to participate in church activities. Her parents were strict, but Carrie respected their wishes. Often she would stay close to home, enjoying her mother's company.

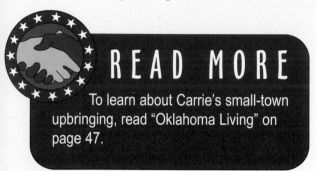

READ MORE

To learn about Carrie's small-town upbringing, read "Oklahoma Living" on page 47.

Carrie might not have been one of the "popular" girls, but she had a good group of caring friends. "We never felt pressure to do anything bad," Carrie said. "Status wasn't that huge a deal in my grade." When she and her friends attended school functions—like the high-school prom—they would hang out afterward to bowl or watch movies.

For Carrie, school was mostly about learning and doing well, and she rarely found herself faced with situations that might get her in trouble. Rather than having to worry about her parents getting angry at her for misbehaving, "I was most afraid of the 'I'm disappointed in you' speech," Carrie recalled. As a straight-A student, however, Carrie did little to disappoint her parents. When she graduated from Checotah High School in May of 2001, she was named class salutatorian.

College Lessons

Throughout high school, Carrie continued to sing in competitions. After she graduated, however, her dream of becoming a professional musician began to slip away. It was time to go to col-

Carole and Carrie Underwood have a particularly close relationship. Carrie has often credited her mother's support for helping her to achieve her dream of a music career.

lege and set her sights on a practical job. Music just seemed too risky and unstable a career.

Carrie decided to major in journalism at Northeastern State University (NSU). NSU was located in the city of Tahlequah, about an hour's drive from Checotah. This meant that Carrie could easily visit home whenever she wished.

As in high school, Carrie worked hard in college. A dedicated journalism student, Carrie joined the school newspaper and worked on a student-produced television program. She did well in her studies and was liked by her teachers. They even gave

Carrie the unusual nickname of Pajama Girl. "[It was] because I would roll out of bed, brush my teeth and go to class," Carrie said. As far as Carrie was concerned, going to college was about learning, not about fashion!

She did get dressed up, however, for several pageants held at NSU in 2002 and 2003. These beauty, talent, and academic pageants gave Carrie an opportunity to receive scholarship money for college. One year, she won First Runner-Up and Overall Talent Winner in the Miss NSU Pageant. Another year, she made it to the top three.

Outside of school, Carrie loved to help animals. She had been a vegetarian since the age of 13 and believed in standing up for animal rights. Carrie also worked at a veterinary clinic. "I don't think enough people stand up for animals," she explained. "My heart goes out to them because, to me, every single animal has a heart and a mind and a soul."

In her personal life, Carrie began to date and develop romantic relationships. She also joined the sorority Sigma Sigma Sigma and became very close with her sorority sisters. These friends encouraged Carrie to keep on singing. Music was no longer Carrie's top priority, but she still enjoyed performing. In the summers, she participated in NSU's Downtown Country Show. These shows were full of singing and dancing, and they gave Carrie a chance to have fun on stage.

When You Least Expect It

By the time Carrie was a senior at NSU, she had basically given up on a music career. Her goal was to graduate and find a job in broadcast journalism. Then, when Carrie least expected it, something happened to change her plans. It all had to do with a little show called *American Idol* and an audition that would transform her life.

CHAPTER THREE

AN IDOL IN THE MAKING

In the summer of 2004, the popular television program *American Idol* began holding auditions for its upcoming fourth season. In cities across the country, tens of thousands of young people showed up to try out for the program. But only 24 talented contestants would eventually make it to the live television show.

Singing in St. Louis

When Carrie learned that one of the auditions would take place in St. Louis, Missouri, she decided to attend. "It was a 'why not?' kind of thing," Carrie said. "'Why not? What do I have to lose, except for gas money?'" It was an opportunity too good to pass up.

Carole agreed to accompany Carrie, and soon, mother and daughter were on the road. The drive from Checotah to St. Louis took seven and a half hours. But as Carrie would soon discover, it was time well spent.

When Carrie and Carole arrived in St. Louis, they waited in line with approximately 10,000 other aspiring singers. Everyone was hoping to be the next American Idol.

One of the most nerve-wracking parts of the audition was singing in front of the *American Idol* judges, Randy Jackson, Paula Abdul, and Simon Cowell. If Carrie could impress the three of them, she would then fly to Hollywood for the next round of auditions.

When it was finally Carrie's turn, she anxiously stepped into the private audition room. For the first few moments, she chatted with the three judges and answered a few of their questions. Then it came time for Carrie to sing.

She chose the song "I Can't Make You Love Me" by Bonnie Raitt. Like all of the other *American Idol* contestants, Carrie had to perform the song a cappella—without any musical accompaniment. As Carrie sang, her voice floated out strong and clear. The judges were thoroughly impressed. They passed her through to the next round of auditions. Carrie Underwood was headed to Hollywood!

A Country Girl in Hollywood

At age 21, Carrie stepped onto a plane for the first time. She was traveling to Los Angeles, where the intense *American Idol* screening process would continue. If Carrie could make it through this second round of tryouts, she would officially become one of the 24 *American Idol* contestants and perform on live television.

For a country girl like Carrie, Hollywood was a big change. Once, when asked whether she had seen any stars, Carrie innocently replied, "It's been pretty cloudy." She didn't realize the question was about famous celebrities, not stars in the sky!

In Hollywood, all of the best singers from prior auditions were now competing against each other. The pressure was on, but Carrie sang well. Finally, it was time for the judges to decide who would move on. Carrie waited anxiously until hearing the good news. She'd made it to the top 24! In a few weeks, she would be singing on one of the most watched television programs in the nation's history.

Carrie Underwood is on the left in this photo of the top 12 finalists from season four of *American Idol*. With her are (left to right) Mario Vasquez, Mikalah Gordon, Constantino Maroulis, Nadia Turner, Bo Bice, Vonzell Solomon, Anthony Federov, Jessica Sierra, Anwar Robinson, Lindsey Cardinale, and Scott Savol.

American Idol Goes Live

On February 22, 2005, Carrie and 11 other female contestants gave their first live performances on *American Idol*. Millions of viewers tuned in to watch. Back in Oklahoma, fans gathered on the NSU campus to cheer and vote for their number-one girl. Carrie's mom, Carole, was among these supporters.

If Carrie was nervous about her live debut, she didn't show it. With grace and poise, she sang "Could've Been" by the artist Tiffany. After she finished, the judges praised her performance. Simon even stated that she should be considered one of the favorites to win the whole competition. It certainly was a promising start.

Because *American Idol* performances were broadcast live, the show followed a precise schedule. Contestants performed on Tuesday nights, and viewers then called to vote for their favorites. On Wednesdays, the voting results were revealed and one unlucky singer was sent home. These eliminations were very stressful, but they were all part of the *American Idol* game.

To prepare for these weekly performances, Carrie rehearsed constantly. She spent hours singing in music studios, practicing with vocal coaches, and running through songs with the *American Idol* band. No one wanted to get eliminated from the competition, and there was tremendous pressure to do well.

READ MORE

Read "The *American Idol* Fashion Scoop" to find out how Carrie looked during the show. Go to page 48.

During each show, Carrie continued to sing her heart out. Sometimes the judges were disappointed by her performances, but viewers kept voting Carrie through to the next round. Then, on March 22, Carrie gave her most electrifying performance yet. On that day, she chose to sing the 1980s classic rock ballad "Alone" by the band Heart. Carrie's performance was so good that judge Simon Cowell delivered a staggering compliment. "Carrie," he said, "you're not just the girl to beat, you're the person to beat. I'll make a prediction: Not only will you win this show, you'll sell more records than any other previous 'Idol' winner." Carrie was astonished. Simon was by far the most critical judge, and contestants could barely dream of receiving such a compliment.

Families, Friends, and Enemies

Competing on the show was very exciting, but it was also emotionally draining. Often, Carrie felt homesick for Oklahoma.

She missed her family and her friends. And she missed her farm and her furry, four-legged pets. It was hard being separated from everything she knew and loved.

Carrie still had fun, however, with her new *American Idol* family. She and the other contestants lived together, shopped together, and laughed together. "When we're with the same people for so long, especially when we're without family and we're without our friends, we have to rely on each other, or we'll go nuts," Carrie said. One of her closest *American Idol* buddies was Anthony Federov. During the ups and downs of the show, the two of them always supported each other. "He's like my brother," Carrie said.

Beyond her *Idol* family, Carrie had the support of millions of fans. Her admirers nicknamed themselves the Care Bears in honor of their favorite *Idol* contestant. All of Oklahoma was crazy for Carrie, and NSU continued to host weekly voting parties. She'd gone from being an unknown college student to a huge celebrity overnight, and millions of Americans were cheering her on.

Staying in the Game

As the weeks went past, more *American Idol* contestants were eliminated. Carrie, however, continued to stay in the game. By May 11, 2005, only three contestants remained: Bo Bice, Vonzell Solomon, and Carrie Underwood. It was a great achievement for all of them to have come this far.

Carrie performs on *American Idol*. The program was one of the top-rated shows of 2005, with each episode drawing approximately 27 million viewers.

To celebrate their accomplishment, each of them briefly returned home for a special town parade. These parades gave local fans a chance to personally cheer for their favorite contestant. They also drummed up excitement for the *American Idol* finale.

In Oklahoma, Carrie's homecoming bash was scheduled for May 13. On that day, Carrie rose very early to give interviews to Tulsa radio stations. From there, she went to Checotah for her celebratory parade. Carrie-mania had taken over as thousands of people flooded the streets. Later that afternoon, she performed "The Star Spangled Banner" and accepted many awards, including the key to the city. Overwhelmed by the show of support, Carrie tearfully thanked the crowd. Now, more than ever, she wanted to win the *American Idol* title.

The Home Stretch

After returning back to Los Angeles, Carrie, Bo, and Vonzell sang in a heated competition on May 17. The very next day, Vonzell was eliminated. Now only Carrie and Bo were left to compete in the show's final episodes.

Many critics believed Bo had the better chance of winning. His easy-going attitude, long hair, and Southern rock sound appealed to many viewers. Carrie, on the other hand, was the all-American girl with the bright smile and the big, bold voice. Both contestants were deserving, but only one could be named the winner.

On May 24, 2005, the final *American Idol* competition took place in Hollywood's famous Kodak Theater. Carrie and Bo each performed three songs to a huge audience of

READ MORE

For information on *American Idol*'s host and judges, read "Ryan, Paula, Randy, and Simon" on page 49.

The season four finalists: Carrie, Bo Bice, and Vonzell Solomon.

cheering fans. Now all that was left was for viewers to vote and determine the season four winner.

The very next night was the *American Idol* finale. This two-hour-long show replayed big moments from season four. It also featured great singing performances and lots of anticipation for

As confetti falls, Carrie performs the song "Inside Your Heaven" after being named the winner of *American Idol*.

the big announcement. Finally, it was time to name the winner. Everyone waited anxiously as Carrie and Bo took center stage. All the members of Carrie's family were in the audience. Then, the show's host, Ryan Seacrest, appeared and opened a golden envelope. Millions of viewers watched and waited as Ryan announced the country's newest Idol: Carrie Underwood!

All of the other *American Idol* contestants rushed onto the stage to give their congratulations. Carrie laughed and cried and hugged everyone. Then she sang one last song on the *American Idol* stage. Confetti rained down as the crowd went wild. It was an incredible moment for Carrie—the first of many to come.

CHAPTER FOUR

ONE WILD YEAR

Only 15 days after being crowned the American Idol, Carrie gave her debut performance at the Grand Ole Opry in Nashville, Tennessee. Since 1925, the Opry had been entertaining audiences with its radio broadcasts and live shows. The Opry stage was legendary in country music, and Carrie was honored to be invited to perform there. She sang "Inside Your Heaven," a song that she had first performed during the finale of *American Idol*. "Inside Your Heaven" would become Carrie's first single.

It was exciting for Carrie to give one of her first post-*Idol* performances at such a respected country music institution. "To be able to perform there and be among all the legends and stars who have come before me was an absolute honor," Carrie said, "and I am very much looking forward to it again. Hopefully one day I can become a member of this amazing organization." For Carrie, her Opry debut was an incredible occasion. But it was just the very beginning of her career. A whirlwind of success was coming her way.

READ MORE

Read "The Grand Ole Opry" on page 50 to learn more about this famous country music institution.

Carrie performs while holding a teddy bear thrown onstage by a fan. The country star's loyal fans call themselves Care Bears.

The Idol Tour

One month later, in July 2005, Carrie went on tour with nine of the other *Idol* performers from season four. The group performed in dozens of cities during their jam-packed summer concert schedule. Touring was fun, but it was also very demanding. When asked, Carrie described a typical day as follows:

> I usually wake up and I think: "OK, now where am
> I right now?" We load up all of our stuff and go do

a show. Then we pack up all of our stuff and head to the next town and do it all over again—check into hotels at like 3, 4 in the morning—and I think we like have a 10-hour drive somewhere.

It was hard work performing week after week. None of the singers had much time to relax. Audiences were grateful to see their favorite stars perform, however, and the *American Idol* concerts were always packed. When the tour arrived in Norman, Oklahoma, Carrie was particularly happy. Over 7,500 of her fans came to this performance. Carrie was touched by their support. For her, it was one of the tour's highlights.

For the last show of the tour, the Idols decided to perform a benefit concert. The proceeds from the show would help the victims of Hurricane Katrina. In August 2005 this deadly storm had devastated parts of Louisiana, Mississippi, and Alabama. Now, the Idols wanted to help those people whose lives had been affected. Proceeds from the concert were sent to the American Red Cross. Carrie also donated her time and money to the Humane Society to help animals affected by the hurricane.

The Making of *Some Hearts*

After the *Idol* tour wrapped in September, Carrie began focusing on her first album, *Some Hearts*. She had started to record the album in the summer of 2005, but her hectic touring schedule made it difficult to get much done. Now that the tour was over, Carrie could work steadily on her album.

The development and recording of *Some Hearts* took place in Nashville. True to character, the album would be country. "There were some people who wanted to push me in a pop direction," Carrie said, "but we sat down and I said, '[Country] is where my heart is. These are the people who voted for me, and they're being so supportive and wonderful. I don't want to abandon who I am at all." Luckily for Carrie, she worked with a team of music professionals who listened to her and respected her wishes.

Many writers and musicians came together to develop the different tracks on the album. Often, the songs that Carrie liked best told interesting stories about people's lives. One example was "Jesus, Take the Wheel." In this song, a young mother finds strength in God when her life nearly spins out of control. When it was released, "Jesus, Take the Wheel" became an instant hit.

Another memorable song on the album was "Don't Forget to Remember Me." The lyrics focused on the loving relationship between a mother and her 18-year-old daughter who is leaving home for the first time. As Carrie explained, this song affected her deeply:

> The first time that I heard it, I cried because I was feeling homesick. I got the lyrics and managed to lose them in a stack of papers that I was sending home. My mother got the package and read through the lyrics. She called me and said that the song made her cry, too, and she only read the words. She said that it was "our song." In that moment, I knew that no matter how hard it would be to get through, I had to record it.

The song made it onto the album and would eventually become another successful single.

One of the last songs on *Some Hearts* was the autobiographical "I Ain't in Checotah Anymore." In this upbeat country song, which Carrie co-wrote, she sang about her Oklahoma roots and the wild new life she was experiencing as a celebrity.

A Sweet November

Some Hearts was scheduled for release in mid-November of 2005. Carrie had worked very hard on the album. Now, her biggest concern was whether it would sell. "The most stress came after my album was done," she said, "and it was kind of like, OK, well this many people voted for me—are they all going to go out and buy an album?" Critics were skeptical. No one knew whether her success on *American Idol* would translate into music sales. All that was left was to wait and find out.

Finally, on November 15, 2005, the album hit the stores. At the 24-hour Wal-Mart in Checotah, customers started buying *Some Hearts* right at midnight. They were very excited to support their hometown girl.

In another part of the country, Carrie herself bought a copy. There she was— a brand new music star—purchasing an album with her face on the cover! It was a surreal moment.

Posters in a record store promote Carrie's first album, *Some Hearts*. To date, the album has sold more than 7 million copies, making it one of the best-selling country music records of all time.

November 15 was important for another reason as well. That day, Carrie was scheduled to perform "Jesus, Take the Wheel" at the 39th annual CMA Awards. It was the first time that she would sing at a huge awards show.

Because Carrie was new to the country music scene, the show's producers only allowed her to sing an abridged version of "Jesus, Take the Wheel." Carrie was disappointed that she couldn't perform the entire song, but she was still grateful for the opportunity to sing. Then, a bad case of the flu hit a few hours before she was supposed to go on stage. Between nerves and a queasy stomach, Carrie wasn't sure if she'd make it through the night. But like the professional she was, she performed the song without a hitch.

Carrie performs during the 2005 "Christmas in Washington" show, an annual event held to raise money for the National Children's Medical Center. Other stars who performed at the event included the country group Rascal Flatts and R&B singer Ciara.

More Success

After just one week in the stores, *Some Hearts* had sold 314,000 copies! This was an amazing sales figure for any singer, especially someone brand new to the music business like Carrie Underwood.

Meanwhile, Carrie was in the midst of moving to Nashville. Even though this city was big, Carrie liked Nashville for its friendly atmosphere. She thought it had small-town charm. Her new house was a comfortable three-bedroom place that would put her close to Nashville's music scene.

After her move, Carrie continued to perform. In between her regular concerts, she did a number of benefit shows, including "Christmas in Washington." This show raised money for the National Children's

Medical Center in Washington, D.C. Carrie also sang at sporting events, such as the all-star games for the National Basketball Association and Major League Baseball.

Carrie's music was making a strong impact, and she was rewarded with numerous honors. At the end of 2005, she was named Oklahoman of the Year. Next, she won three *Billboard* Music Awards. These were followed by more honors from the Gospel Music Association and Country Music Television.

Then, on May 23, 2006, the reputable Academy of Country Music (ACM) gave Carrie two more awards. The first was for Single Record of the Year for "Jesus, Take the Wheel." The second was for Top New Female Vocalist. Carrie was honored to receive such recognition from the well-respected ACM. It was yet another symbol of her continued success.

READ MORE

Read "V Is for Vegetarian" to learn more about Carrie's lifestyle, as well as her involvement with animal organizations. Go to page 51.

A College Grad

Music was obviously Carrie's main priority. But a college education was still very important to her, too. When Carrie entered the *American Idol* competition, she was only one semester short of graduating. Rather than give up on her degree, Carrie worked out a plan with her professors to complete her studies. On May 6, 2006, Carrie graduated from Northeastern State University with 1,800 other students.

"It was important to me to finish school," Carrie said. "My parents had invested so much that I thought they deserved to see me walk across the stage at graduation. And someday, when I'm telling my kids they need to go to college, I'll know

Carrie proudly accepts her diploma during the graduation ceremony at Northeastern State University, May 2006.

what I'm talking about." Carrie graduated magna cum laude with a Bachelor of Arts degree in mass communications and journalism.

The Music Keeps on Flowing

In the summer of 2006, Carrie geared up for more performances. In June, she participated in Nashville's CMA Music Festival. Then, in July, she went on her first big country music tour, opening for superstar Kenny Chesney. As Carrie racked up more performances, it was common to find the singer at concerts performing with the likes of Randy Travis, Keith Urban, and Brad Paisley.

Again and again, Carrie was proving herself as a singer. "I was built for this," she said. "I feel like everyone has a destiny, a path they're supposed to be on." Now Carrie was trailblazing her way into country music history. And her career was only going to get better and better.

CHAPTER FIVE

FACING THE FUTURE

In the fall of 2006, Carrie Underwood continued to find success. Her album *Some Hearts* had sold millions of copies, and her list of awards was growing. In December, she took home five *Billboard* Music Awards. The star was proud of her accomplishments. But there was one thing she still hoped to find—a bit of romance to spice up her life.

Hanging Out with the Boys

In college, Carrie described herself as "one of those girls who was always in a relationship." She'd dated fellow NSU student Drake Clark during her days on *American Idol*. But this relationship eventually ended. Later, she went out with another Oklahoma friend, Chad Eagleton. But several months later, they also broke up. Carrie was realizing how difficult it was to date with such a demanding new career.

Then, in December of 2006, Carrie was spotted with football quarterback Tony Romo of the Dallas Cowboys. Quickly, rumors spread that the two were dating. Carrie, however, insisted they were just good friends. She and Tony cared for each other, but a serious romance was never part of the picture.

In her life, Carrie has said that she often feels closer to men than women:

> I definitely have more guy friends. I'm not a huge talker. And hanging out with guys, you don't really have to talk. My guy friends and I can watch three hours of TV and not say a word, and that's cool. I like playing old-school Nintendo. I love football and I love guy movies. I hate getting flowers, and I hate chick flicks. That whole romance thing—that doesn't happen. Real guys aren't like that.

As for a boyfriend, Carrie would just have to wait for the right person to come along. For now, she said, she would stay single and enjoy the life of an independent woman.

A Whirlwind of Awards

During 2006, Carrie performed at over 150 shows. These performances took her all around the globe. Sometimes, she sang close to home in Nashville. Other times, she criss-crossed the United States. During the Christmas holidays, she even traveled to Kuwait and Iraq to sing for U.S. troops stationed there.

At home, Carrie's trophy case was filling up quickly. In three months, she pulled in 10 awards: two Country Music Association Awards, one American Music Award, five *Billboard* Music Awards, and two People's Choice Awards. Then, on February 11, 2007, Carrie added two Grammys to her collection—one for Best

READ MORE

If you want to learn more about the prestigious Grammy Awards, go to "The Grammys" on page 52.

Carrie sits with Dallas Cowboys quarterback Tony Romo at an awards show in May 2007. Although newspaper stories speculated that the two were dating, Carrie maintained that they were just good friends.

Female Country Vocal Performance for "Jesus, Take the Wheel" and another for Best New Artist.

Many critics were particularly impressed that Carrie had won the Grammy for Best New Artist. Because this award is open to all new artists—not just country singers—Carrie had to compete against nominees with backgrounds in pop, R&B, alternative, and soul. By winning Best New Artist, Carrie

In December 2006, Carrie visited American soldiers in Iraq and Kuwait as part of a USO tour. The USO enlists popular performers to entertain U.S. troops stationed around the world. Here, Carrie performs a concert for the troops in Tikrit, Iraq.

proved that she could hold her own against artists in any musical genre.

Performing on Television

Following the Grammys, Carrie appeared as the musical guest on the comedy show *Saturday Night Live* (*SNL*). Only four country music stars had ever performed on *SNL* since this show first started in 1975. Now, Carrie was honored as the fifth. "*Saturday Night Live* was really cool," she said. "It was great to be added to the list of such great iconic artists who have performed on the show before."

Carrie sang two songs that night: "Wasted" and "Before He Cheats." Performing on *SNL* gave Carrie a chance to reach millions of mainstream viewers—not just country music fans.

A few weeks later, Carrie appeared on another television show, *Idol Gives Back*. This special program was created to raise money for charities in the United States and Africa. For this event, Carrie recorded a version of the Pretenders' song "I'll Stand by You." Proceeds from the sale of this song went to various charities. Carrie also made a trip to South Africa to perform for kids and adults alike. There, she saw people living with disease and poverty. It was an experience that opened her eyes to the many problems in the world.

In her own life, Carrie felt that she was very blessed. "I totally believe that my voice came from God. That's where my talent comes from. I always want to make sure that I give back any way I can." Carrie was true to her word. She continued to participate in more charity events and help others—both people and animals—whenever she could.

Carnival Ride

By the beginning of 2007, Carrie's album *Some Hearts* had sold more than 5 million copies. It was an incredible figure that made Carrie proud. But the success of *Some Hearts* was also daunting as she began working on her second album, *Carnival Ride*:

> "Is there really anywhere to go but down?" There was that fear in my head. Then we started picking songs and I realized it was more [about] making an album for myself that I love and I know I have a huge hand in making. Whatever happens, it's icing on the cake.

For *Carnival Ride*, Carrie took her time working on the material. She and her team sifted through tons of great songs, choosing only the best for her album. Carrie also developed her own talent as a songwriter. On *Some Hearts*, she co-wrote just one song. But on *Carnival Ride*, she co-wrote four. Carrie explained how the lyrics of one of these songs, "Wheel of the World," inspired the album's title:

> My favorite line on the whole album pretty much sums up everything that I've been through . . . "God put us here on this carnival ride/We close our eyes never knowing where it will take us

next." It's beautiful and so true. We don't know what we're doing or where we're headed. We just kind of trust and hope that whatever ride we're on in life takes us where we need to go.

In Carrie's life, her own personal carnival ride was a journey full of surprises. On October 23, 2007, *Carnival Ride* was released. In its first week in stores, *Carnival Ride* sold 527,000 copies—an incredible number. A few months earlier, Carrie had released her first single from the album, "So Small." Now that song was topping the radio charts. Two other songs—"All-American Girl" and "Last Name"—were soon to follow. Once again, Carrie had proven that she was a rising star of country music.

Tabloids, Tours, and Television

In her personal life, Carrie began dating actor Chace Crawford from the television series *Gossip Girl*. The tabloids regularly reported on their romance, but Carrie tried to downplay the relationship. For now, she was interested in having fun and keeping things light. Their relationship lasted for a couple of months.

Carrie's career was still her primary focus. Every week, she made headlines with her performances and award wins. Fans could hear her music on the radio, see her videos on Country Music Television, or watch her attending the latest awards shows. Her music even made it to the silver screen when she recorded an original song for the Disney movie *Enchanted*. To end 2007, she performed at *Dick Clark's New Year's Rockin' Eve* show. This blowout celebration was held in Times Square and marked the end to another year.

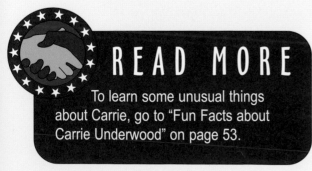

READ MORE

To learn some unusual things about Carrie, go to "Fun Facts about Carrie Underwood" on page 53.

In 2007, Carrie maintained a hectic schedule of touring and recording.

Carrie started the new year with a bang by winning her third Grammy. Then, she began touring with singer Keith Urban to promote *Carnival Ride*. This collaboration was fun for Carrie. "Keith and I are a good mix," she said. "He's obviously extremely talented and plays guitar like no other."

In between these concert shows, Carrie still found time for other activities. She appeared again on *Saturday Night Live* and

Country music legend Garth Brooks presented Carrie Underwood for induction into the prestigious Grand Ole Opry on May 10, 2008. During the evening, Carrie sang three of her hits for the Opry audience.

the charity event *Idol Gives Back*. But one of the biggest events of her life took place on May 10, 2008—the day Carrie Underwood became a member of the Grand Ole Opry.

New Year, New Horizons

On the night of her Opry induction, Carrie performed "All-American Girl" to a sold-out Opry House. Then, singer Garth Brooks presented Carrie with the very special Opry Member Award. "Nothing will last as long or be more important than this award right here tonight," Garth said. "Congratulations." Carrie took her award and kissed it. As a little girl, she had dreamed of one day singing on the Opry stage. Now, at age 25, Carrie had joined the most celebrated and respected country music institution in history. It was the achievement of a lifetime.

In November 2008, Carrie Underwood won the CMA's Female Vocalist of the Year award for the third consecutive time. The superstar also co-hosted the show with country singer Brad Paisley.

To date, Carrie's two albums have sold over 9 million copies. She's performed at hundreds of shows and received countless awards. Her beautiful voice and professionalism make her one of country music's greatest stars. And her music will surely continue to make an impact—both within the country music community and the world at large.

The Country Music Association

Since 1958, the Country Music Association (CMA) has promoted country music throughout the world. More than 5,500 music professionals are part of the CMA, including artists, producers, radio station staff, and talent agents. Their work helps county music thrive and grow.

The CMA hosts several impressive music events every year. One of those events is the annual CMA Awards. Winners are selected by the CMA members, who vote through a series of ballots. Some famous award winners include Carrie Underwood, the Dixie Chicks, Keith Urban, and Johnny Cash.

During the awards ceremony, the CMA also inducts a few artists into the Country Music Hall of Fame. The Hall of Fame museum has been a part of Nashville since the 1960s. It celebrates the history and vibrancy of country music.

In the summer, the CMA also hosts the incredible CMA Music Festival. This Nashville extravaganza brings together hundreds of artists and thousands of fans for four days of country music. Artists donate their time for free, performing, signing autographs, and posing for pictures. The event also raises money for "Keep the Music Playing," a music education program for Nashville's children.

The Country Music Association promotes country music throughout the world.

The Lowdown on "Before He Cheats"

With her big brown eyes and country-girl charm, Carrie Underwood's got the wholesome look of an American sweetheart. But don't let looks fool you. This superstar has plenty of sass and brass—at least as far as her music goes.

When Carrie's song "Before He Cheats" first came out, it surprised many listeners. There was nothing sweet or innocent about it. The song was about getting revenge on a cheating boyfriend by destroying his car. The chorus went, "I dug my key into the side/Of his pretty little souped-up four-wheel drive/Carved my name into his leather seat/I took a Louisville slugger to both head lights/Slashed a hole in all four tires/And maybe next time he'll think before he cheats."

The feisty song instantly became a hit, but in an interview Carrie made it clear that she did not approve of the lyrics' violent message:

> I decided to sing ["Before He Cheats"] because I think that everyone has a "mean streak," and the character in the song has a very large one. I would like to say, however, that I do not condone the destruction of anyone's property and I have never, at any time, keyed anyone's car.

Turns out Carrie is still a good girl at heart—even if she acts bad in the make-believe world of her music.

Carrie belts out "Before He Cheats" at the 2007 Country Music Television awards show. The song is the biggest hit of Carrie's career so far.

Country Music 101

Country music's roots sprang from the mostly mountainous region in the eastern United States known as Appalachia. Most of Appalachia stretches from southern New York state at its northern end through parts of Pennsylvania, Ohio, West Virginia, Maryland, Virginia, Kentucky, Tennessee, and North Carolina into northern Mississippi, Alabama, Georgia, and South Carolina, at its southernmost point. There, in those southern regions of Appalachia, singers performed using stringed instruments such as guitars, fiddles, and banjos. Many of these musicians were influenced by the music of their English, Scottish, and Irish ancestors. Country music was also shaped by the jazz and blues melodies of African Americans. During the 1920s, some radio stations began playing country music on the air.

In the 1930s, cowboy movies increased the popularity of country music. As this music spread throughout the United States, more artists developed new kinds of country sounds. There were the dance-driven songs of Western Swing, the banjo music of Bluegrass, and the down-and-out songs of Honky Tonk.

From the 1940s to the 1970s, stars like Hank Williams, Patsy Cline, and Willie Nelson pushed country music to the forefront. In more recent decades, country artists have merged country and pop sounds together. In the future, country music will surely continue to change and grow.

Jimmie Rodgers (1897–1933) is sometimes called the "father of country music"

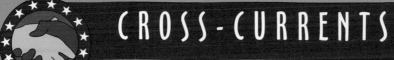

Oklahoma Living

Carrie Underwood loved growing up on a farm in Checotah, Oklahoma. But if anyone ever made false assumptions about her rural upbringing, Carrie was quick to correct them:

> No, we don't have milk cows. People have so many stereotypes of people from where I come from. If you say you're from Oklahoma, it'll be like, "Oh, so you milk cows, feed chickens, ride bulls, all that stuff, right?" And it's like: "No. We don't ride around in covered wagons, either."

Carrie's family raised cattle—one of Oklahoma's main forms of agriculture. (Carrie herself is a vegetarian, but she still helped her father around the farm by feeding and taking care of the animals.) In the town itself, there was just one traffic light. Carrie got her hair cut at a beauty salon that was located inside a hardware store.

Checotah wasn't a cosmopolitan hub. But it made Carrie the strong woman that she is today. "Me being from where I'm from is a big part of my success," Carrie has said. She is proud to be an Oklahoma native and a small-town girl.

CROSS-CURRENTS

The *American Idol* Fashion Scoop

On *American Idol*, singing is clearly the main priority. But looking good is important, too. This is why a team of hair, makeup, and fashion stylists work with all of the contestants. "You're in front of millions of people, and you do have to make an impression and look your absolute best," explains Miles Siggins, the show's fashion stylist.

During season four, Carrie had a mix of *Idol* fashion hits and misses. "It's been a big learning curve for Carrie," Miles said. "In the beginning, she was very country. She grew up on a farm, and she's had no exposure to fashion. Where she's from, the local supermarket doesn't even sell *Elle* or *Vogue*."

Each week, Carrie was given a clothing budget to go shopping. But this country girl admitted she was too practical to spend her money on fashionable but expensive clothes:

> I was saving every penny I could from any money I got from the show. I thought, "I'll put this away, and I can go finish college after it's over," because I never expected to win. My thoughts were, "There's no way I'm going to drop 800 bucks on a dress." That's silly.

> Who knew that after winning *American Idol*, this country girl would have the chance to wear designer dresses costing hundreds of thousands of dollars!

A stylist works on Carrie's hair before an episode of *American Idol*.

Ryan, Paula, Randy, and Simon

What makes *American Idol* such a television phenomenon? Many people think it's the contestants. But a big part of *Idol*'s success is due to the personalities of four people who are identified with the show: Ryan Seacrest, Randy Jackson, Paula Abdul, and Simon Cowell.

Ryan, the show's host, always has a way of putting people at ease. Confident and charming, Ryan knows how to work a crowd. Today, he is one of the biggest entertainment moguls in Hollywood.

American Idol's judges are another important part of the show. One judge, Randy Jackson, worked as a musician and music producer for over 20 years. On *Idol*, Randy is famous for his colorful and honest critiques. Contestants know they've done a good job when Randy calls their performances "hot."

Before appearing on *American Idol*, Paula Abdul was famous as a pop singer and a dance choreographer. Now, as a judge, she is known for giving kind and gentle critiques, even if a performance is less than perfect.

Simon Cowell is the most abrasive of the judges. Viewers count on Simon to deliver blunt and harsh criticism. A compliment from him is often rare, but well deserved. Outside of *Idol*, Simon works in music and television as a producer and talent scout.

The popular *Idol* personalities: Randy Jackson, Paula Abdul, Ryan Seacrest, and Simon Cowell.

The Grand Ole Opry

The Grand Ole Opry originated in 1925 as a country music radio broadcast. These weekly programs aired from Nashville. Fans of the show began coming to the radio station to watch the musicians perform. Eventually, a 500-person auditorium was built to accommodate these audiences. As more people arrived to see the show, however, the managers of the Opry realized they needed a bigger location.

For several years, the Opry moved from place to place. Then in 1943, it found its home at the Ryman Auditorium. Many great performers played at the Ryman, making it one of the most famous venues for country music.

During the 1970s, the Opry moved again, this time to the Opry House. In the center of the Opry House stage, builders included a six-foot circle of polished wood taken from the Ryman Auditorium. This circle honors the Ryman's history and all of the amazing musicians who performed there.

Today, the Opry represents the crown jewel of country music. Fans still listen to the radio broadcasts, and audiences flock to see the Opry House shows. To sing on this stage is a huge honor, and to become an Opry member is an even bigger achievement.

Country music's greatest stars have performed at Grand Ole Opry in Nashville.

CROSS-CURRENTS

V Is for Vegetarian

In 2005 and 2007, Carrie Underwood was voted World's Sexiest Vegetarian! The group People for the Ethical Treatment of Animals (PETA) sponsored the online voting process. Other celebrities who have won this honor include Prince, Kristin Bell, Andre 3000, and Shania Twain.

How did fans first realize that Carrie is a vegetarian? Many people found out when she wore a special "V Is for Vegetarian" t-shirt while bowling with her *American Idol* buddies. Since then, Carrie has been known for sporting similar t-shirts during her concerts.

Carrie stopped eating meat when she was about 13 years old. Today she is an animal activist and a member of the Humane Society of the United States. In Humane Society ads, Carrie has encouraged people to spay and neuter their pets. By doing this simple and inexpensive task, she explains, pet owners can reduce the number of homeless animals born into the world.

Carrie herself is a huge pet lover. She grew up surrounded by many different animals and took care of a stray cat in college. Now in Nashville, Carrie showers her affection on a cute little dog named Ace. Whenever Carrie has to travel, she brings Ace with her as often as she can.

Carrie, photographed here with several adorable puppies, is a vegetarian and animal activist.

CROSS-CURRENTS

The Grammys

Since 1959, the National Academy of Recording Arts and Sciences of the United States has hosted the annual Grammy Awards. These awards recognize achievements in music. The award itself is a small statuette made in the shape of a gramophone. Unlike other music awards, the Grammys are not based on music sales or radio airplay. Instead, members of the Academy vote to choose the Grammy nominees and winners.

The Grammys recognize a range of musical genres—from country to pop to classical to reggae. In the past, new or developing genres have also been added to the Grammy list. In 1980, the Academy included rock as a new genre. In 1989, rap was added. In awarding Grammys, the National Academy of Recording Arts and Sciences strives to keep up-to-date with the trends and changes in music.

Most of the Grammy Awards cover specific genres of music. For example, there are awards specifically for pop artists and awards specifically for country artists. But four general awards are open to all types of music. These awards are Record of the Year, Album of the Year, Song of the Year, and Best New Artist. Many people consider these general awards to be the most important and prestigious of the Grammys.

Carrie poses with the Grammy Award for Best Female Country Vocal Performance, which she received in February 2008.

Fun Facts about Carrie Underwood

Things you never knew about Carrie:

- She loves horror movies like *Friday the 13th* and *A Nightmare on Elm Street*. She's also a big fan of the show *Star Trek: The Next Generation*.

- During her *American Idol* audition in St. Louis, she clucked like a chicken in front of the judges.

- The chocolate company Hershey's hired Carrie to sing its jingles and appear in its commercials.

- Carrie posed for a "Read, Y'all" poster as part of Oklahoma's literacy campaign. These posters were given away for free to Oklahoma libraries and schools.

- Carrie's Nashville house is full of European antiques.

- To stay healthy and slim, Carrie uses a food diary. She writes down all of the things she eats to keep track of the calories, fat, and fiber that she ingests each day.

- Whenever Carrie performs, her Care Bear fans like to throw stuffed bears onto the stage.

- Since winning season four of *American Idol*, Carrie has gone back to the show every year to perform and support the new crop of contestants.

- In a 2008 poll from AOL Television, Carrie was chosen as the most popular American Idol. She won with 54 percent of the vote. The next runner-up, with 26 percent of the vote, was the winner of the first season, Kelly Clarkson.

Carrie Underwood received a "sweet deal"—a deal to endorse Hershey's chocolate products.

Chronology

1983: Carrie Marie Underwood is born on March 10.

2001: graduates from Checotah High School in May.

2004: auditions for season four of *American Idol* in St. Louis, Missouri.

2005: Carrie wins *American Idol* on May 25; releases her first album, *Some Hearts*, on November 15.

2006: graduates from Northeastern State University on May 6; wins her first two awards from the Academy of Country Music on May 23; wins two awards from the Country Music Association on November 6.

2007: Carrie wins her first two Grammys on February 11; appears on *Saturday Night Live* on March 24; *Carnival Ride* released on October 23.

2008: Carrie becomes a member of the Grand Ole Opry on May 10; in November, she is named the CMA's Female Vocalist of the Year for the third straight time.

Accomplishments/Awards
Number One Country Hits

"Inside Your Heaven," 2005
"Jesus, Take the Wheel," 2005
"Before He Cheats," 2005
"Wasted," 2005
"So Small," 2007
"All-American Girl," 2007
"Last Name," 2008
"Just a Dream," 2008

Selected Awards

Gospel Music Association's Dove Award, Country Recorded
 Song of the Year: "Jesus, Take the Wheel," 2006
Academy of Country Music Award, Top New Female Vocalist,
 2006
Academy of Country Music Award, Single Record of the Year:
 "Jesus, Take the Wheel," 2006
Country Music Association Award, Horizon Award, 2006
Country Music Association Award, Female Vocalist of the Year,
 2006
American Music Award, Favorite Breakthrough Artist, 2006
People's Choice Award, Favorite Female Singer, 2007
People's Choice Award, Favorite Country Song: "Before He
 Cheats," 2007

Grammy Award, Best Female Country Vocal Performance: "'Jesus, Take the Wheel," 2007

Grammy Award, Best New Artist, 2007

Academy of Country Music Award, Top Female Vocalist, 2007

Academy of Country Music Award, Album of the Year: "Some Hearts," 2007

Country Music Association Award, Single of the Year: "Before He Cheats," 2007

Country Music Association Award, Female Vocalist of he Year, 2007

American Music Award, Favorite Female Country Artist, 2007

American Music Award, Favorite Country Album: "Some Hearts," 2007

Grammy Award, Best Female Country Vocal Performance: "Before He Cheats," 2008

Academy of Country Music, Top Female Vocalist, 2008

Country Music Association Award, Female Vocalist of the Year, 2008

Further Reading

Jodi Bryson, "As Fate Would Have It," *Girls' Life* (June/July 2006), pp. 40–43, 81, 83.

Laura La Bella. *Carrie Underwood*. New York: Rosen, 2008.

Deborah Evans Price and Ken Tucker, "Carrie Enjoys The Ride," *Billboard* (September 8, 2007), pp. 26–28, 30.

Kathleen Tracy, *Carrie Underwood*. Hockessin, Del.: Mitchell Lane Publishers, 2006.

Kathryn Jenson White, "Carrie Me Home," *Oklahoma Today* 56, no. 1 (January/February 2006), pp. 38–45.

Internet Resources

http://www.carrieunderwoodofficial.com

Carrie Underwood's official Web site includes updated news, music songs and videos, touring information, and fun facts for fans.

http://www.billboard.com/bbcom/bio/index.jsp?pid=657654

The music industry news source *Billboard* provides information on Carrie Underwood, including her biography, discography, and chart history.

http://www.americanidol.com/contestants/season4/carrie_underwood

American Idol's official Web site provides information on Carrie Underwood and video links to her interviews and performances.

http://www.people.com/people/carrie_underwood

The news magazine *People* offers up-to-date biographical information on Carrie Underwood.

http://www.myspace.com/carrieunderwood

Carrie Underwood's MySpace page offers music, news, and touring information.

Glossary

abridged—shortened or condensed.

album—a recorded collection of songs performed by an artist or artists and issued as an individual item.

ballad—a slow song, often about love and romance.

cosmopolitan—sophisticated and worldly; advanced and up-to-date, due to the influence of many cultures.

debut—an artist's first performance.

demo—a sample of recorded music that is used to demonstrate an artist's talent.

finale—the last episode, performance, or scene of a show.

genre—a category or type of art with specific features and traits. In music, country, rock, rap, and R&B are considered different genres.

forum—a place where people can come together to express their thoughts and ideas.

induction—the act of accepting someone into a group or organization.

magna cum laude—a Latin term used to identify college students who graduate with excellent academic grades; the term literally means "with great praise."

mogul—a successful or powerful person who works in the media.

nominate—to recommend someone for an award or a special position.

salutatorian—a student who graduates with the second highest academic score in his or her class.

season—a specific period of time when a television show appears on the air.

sorority—a college social society, open only to female students; members of a sorority typically hang out together.

track—an individual song on an album.

Chapter Notes

p. 10: "Two years ago..." *40th Annual CMA Awards*, first broadcast on November 6, 2006 by ABC.

p. 11: "The idea that I would act..." "Faith Hill Says Angry Reaction Was Just a Joke," *Los Angeles Times* (November 8, 2006), p. E3.

p. 11: "Country radio, the fans..." Keith Groller, "From Country Girl to Country Star: Carrie Underwood Is Still Learning the Headliner Ropes," *Allentown Morning Call*, August 12, 2006, p. 1D.

p. 12: "She is wonderful..." "Take 5: Carrie Underwood," *The Journal Gazette*, December 6, 2005, p. 8D.

p. 12: "I definitely was a tomboy..." Alanna Nash, "America's Idol," *Reader's Digest*, June 2006. http://www.rd.com/celebrities/music-icons/american-idol-carrie-under-wood-interview/article26895.html.

p. 13: "One of my earliest memories..." Shirley Halperin, "Carrie: Success is the Best Revenge," *Teen People*, September 2006, p. 84.

p. 13: "When I was little..." "Idol Chatter," *Tulsa World*, April 14, 2005, p. 3D.

p. 14: "I didn't need to win..." Jodi Bryson, "As Fate Would Have It," *Girls' Life*, June/July 2006, p. 40.

p. 15: "I honestly think..." Matt Gleason, "Coming Clean," *Tulsa World*, March 20, 2005, p. 3H.

p. 16: "We never felt pressure..." Mike Lipton and Darla Atlas, "Homecoming Queen," *People*, November 14, 2005, p. 147.

p. 16: "I was most afraid..." Halperin, "Carrie: Success is the Best Revenge," p. 84.

p. 18: "[It was] because I would..." "Carrie Underwood," *People*, November 2006, p. 38.

p. 18: "I don't think enough..." Nash, "America's Idol."

p. 19: "It was a 'why not?' kind of thing..." John Wooley, "Carrie Okie," *Tulsa World*, August 7, 2005, p. H1.

p. 20: "It's been pretty cloudy." "Bring It On," *People*, February 28, 2005, pp. 88–90.

p. 22: "Carrie, you're not just..." John Wooley and Mike Hughes, "'Idol' Chatter," *Tulsa World*, March 24, 2005, p. 3D.

p. 23: "When we're with the same..." Wooley, "Carrie On!" *Tulsa World*, May 22, 2005, p. H1.

p. 23: "He's like my brother." Wooley, "Carrie On!," p. H1.

p. 27: "To be able to perform..." The Grand Ole Opry Official Web site, "Grand Ole Opry to Reveal Unforgettable Moments of 2005 During 'America's Grand Ole Opry Weekend Year-End Special' Hosted by Dierks Bentley," December 2, 2005. http://www.opry.com/OpryNews/PressRelease.aspx?id=1603.

p. 28: "I usually wake up..." Chris Macias, "Some 'Idol' Thoughts: Country-Singing Carrie Underwood Talks about Her Life on the Road and as a Star," *The Sacramento Bee*, August 19, 2005, p. 14TK.

p. 29: "There were some people..." Scott Mervis, "Music Preview: First She Won 'American Idol.' Next Up for Carrie Underwood: Country Stardom," *Pittsburgh Post-Gazette*, September 1, 2005, p. 20WE.

p. 30: "The first time..." Adrian Gomez, "Rising Star Underwood Keeps Feet on the Ground," *Albuquerque Journal*, September 8, 2006, p. 14.

p. 31: "The most stress came..." Jack Leaver, "Country Sensation; 'American Idol' Winner to Perform in GR This Weekend," *The Grand Rapids Press*, June 1, 2006, p. 24.

p. 33: "It was important to me..." Chad Jones, "'Idol' Carrie Underwood Finds Hits on Her Country Road," *Oakland Tribune*, June 9, 2006, p. 1.

p. 34: "I was built for this..." Bryson, "As Fate Would Have It," p. 40.

p. 35: "One of those girls..." Carissa Rosenberg, "Carrie Underwood," *Seventeen*, November 2007, p. 92.

p. 36: "I definitely have more..." Rosenberg, "Carrie Underwood," p. 92.

p. 38: "Saturday Night Live was..." Carrie Underwood's official Web site. http://www.carrieunderwoodofficial.com/biography.

p. 39: "I totally believe..." Matt Gleason, "Coming Clean," *Tulsa World*, March 20, 2005, p. 3H.

p. 39: "Is there really anywhere..." Deborah Evans Price, " Underwood Tries for Encore with 'Carnival Ride,'" *Billboard*, August 31, 2007. http://www.billboard.com/bbcom/esearch/article_display.jsp?vnu_content_id= 1003633931.

p. 39: "My favorite line..." Price, "Underwood Tries for Encore with 'Carnival Ride.'"

p. 41: "Keith and I..." Tad Dickens, "It's Carrie Underwood's Time to Shine: Grammy Winner Carrie Underwood Has Sustained Success Beyond the 'Sophomore Jinx,'" *The Roanoke Times*, February 15, 2008. http://www.roanoke.com/extra/ wb/150816.

p. 43: "Nothing will last..." Grand Ole Opry Official Web site, "Carrie Underwood Inducted As Newest Member of the Opry by Garth Brooks," May 13, 2008. http://www.opry.com/OpryNews/Headline.aspx?id=6415.

p. 45: "I dug my key..." Chris Tompkins and Josh Kear, "Before He Cheats," performed by Carrie Underwood, Arista Records, 2005.

p. 45: "I decided to sing..." The Internet Archive, Carrie Underwood's Official Web site (May, 14 2006). http://web.archive.org/web/20060514052428/http:// www.carrieunderwoodofficial.com.

p. 47: "No, we don't have milk cows..." Matt Pais, "'Idol' Worship: Carrie Underwood Confronts Internet Admirers and Marriage Proposals," *Chicago Tribune*, August 3, 2005, p. 33.

p. 47: "Me being from where I'm from..." Kathryn Jenson White, "Carrie Me Home," *Oklahoma Today*, January/February 2006, p. 45.

p. 48: "You're in front of..." Anne Bratskeir, "Cool 2 Wear," *Newsday*, May 23, 2005, p. 2B.

p. 48: "It's been a big..." Bratskeir, "Cool 2 Wear," p. 2B.

p. 48: "I was saving..." Bryson, "As Fate Would Have It," p. 40.

Index

Numbers in **bold italics** refer to captions.

Photo Credits

About the Author

MARIKA JEFFERY has worked as an editor and writer for many years. She received her Master's in Children's Literature and specializes in publications for children and young adults. She lives in San Diego with her husband, Keven.